D0754398

UNDERSTANDING
DRUGS

UPFRONT HEALTH

Published in the United States of America by Cherry Lake Publishing
Ann Arbor, Michigan
www.cherrylakepublishing.com

Reading Adviser: Marla Conn MS, Ed., Literacy specialist, Read-Ability, Inc.

Photo Credits: ©Lipik Stock Media/Shutterstock, cover, ©Towfiqu Photography/Getty Images, 1, ©EyeEm/Getty Images, 5, ©iStockphoto/Getty Images, 9, ©, BBM, 11, ©By cheapbooks/Shutterstock, 13, ©sturti/Getty Images, 15, ©iStockphoto/Getty Images, 19, ©Caiaimage/Getty Images, 21, ©http://rebcenter-moscow.ru/, Wikimedia, 22, ©Hero Images/Getty Images, 25, ©Brian C. Weed/Shutterstock, 27, ©iStockphoto/Getty Images, 29, ©Caiaimage/Getty Images, 30

Library of Congress Cataloging-in-Publication Data has been filed and is available at catalog.loc.gov

Cherry Lake Publishing would like to acknowledge the work of The Partnership for 21st Century Learning.
Please visit *www.p21.org* for more information.

Printed in the United States of America
Corporate Graphics

ABOUT THE AUTHOR

Renae Gilles is an author, editor, and ecologist from the Pacific Northwest. She has a bachelor's degree in humanities from Evergreen State College and a master's in biology from Eastern Washington University. Renae and her husband currently live in the Northeast with their two daughters, dog, and flock of backyard chickens.

TABLE OF CONTENTS

CHAPTER 1

The World of Drugs

There are many different types of **drugs** in the world. Some drugs are legal, such as coffee and aspirin. Some are illegal, such as cocaine. Others are legal for people to use at a certain age, such as alcohol. But all drugs can be dangerous. Drugs change the way people think, feel, and act. Even using a small amount of drugs can lead to **abuse** and **addiction**.

Drugs have been used for centuries. Drugs were often used by priests or shamans for spiritual and religious reasons. They were used by healers as medicine. Many drugs were used by people in a socially approved way. This includes many drugs people still use, such as alcohol, tobacco, and coffee. Over time, people started to make these drugs more powerful. Drugs also became easier to use. With these

No one tries drugs with the goal of becoming addicted. But for many people, casual drug use begins a battle with addiction that consumes their lives.

changes, drug abuse and addiction became more common.

When most people think of drugs, they think of illicit drugs. Illicit means the drugs are illegal or frowned upon by society. Today's illicit drugs include marijuana, opium, cocaine, and heroin. Club drugs, LSD, and abused prescription pills are also illicit drugs. Today, the most common illicit drugs are marijuana and prescription pain relievers. About 1 in 10 Americans aged 12 and older use illicit drugs. Rates are higher in young adults. About 1 in 4 people ages 18 to 25 use drugs.

Legalization

Laws concerning drugs have been changing a lot in recent years. This includes marijuana. Many people are in support of marijuana being legal. At first, many states allowed marijuana for medical use. Marijuana can help people with pain and nausea. Recently, some states have made marijuana completely legal. Adults can purchase and use marijuana like they would other substances, such as tobacco or alcohol. Why do you think these places are changing their laws? What might be the impact of the changes?

Most Americans use illicit drugs as a way to relieve pain, outside of the guidance of a doctor. Many young adults use them to feel good or get **high**. Or they want to relax and relieve stress or tension. Some people try these drugs just to see what they are like.

Trying or using drugs to feel good and have fun can lead to addiction. First, someone tries a drug. Then they begin to abuse the drug. Their brain becomes used to having the drug in their body. Then the person starts to lose control of their use. They

[21ST CENTURY SKILLS LIBRARY]

might develop substance use **disorder** (SUD). In the United States, about 7.4 million people ages 12 and older have illicit drug use disorder. More than half of these people have problems with marijuana. About a quarter have problems with prescription pills.

Drugs in School

*Most schools in the United States have a zero-**tolerance** policy for drugs. This means there are very strict rules about drugs at school. A certain punishment is usually included in one of the rules. The punishment is always very strict. A student might be suspended or expelled. Students are afraid of the strict punishment, so they behave. Some people argue that zero-tolerance policies do not work. Strict rules and punishments might not stop students from doing drugs. It might make them dislike school and their teachers instead. Another idea is for schools to focus on support programs. These programs would work with students individually. A student who brought drugs to school would not be punished. They would receive counseling and drug education instead. How are these approaches similar? How are they different? Which do you think would work best?*

CHAPTER 2

The Effects of Drugs

There are many different types of illicit drugs. Each comes with its own effects on the body and mind. Each illicit drug also comes with its own level of addiction. First, a drug is put into the body. Certain drugs are smoked or inhaled. Other drugs are swallowed or injected. The drug enters the bloodstream. The heart then pumps the blood to the brain. When the blood reaches the brain, the effects of the drug are felt.

Marijuana and opioids, such as heroin and opium, create a sense of **euphoria**. They make someone feel relaxed and drowsy. Marijuana also reduces coordination, reflexes, and reaction times. It makes some people anxious and paranoid. Heroin and opium are very addictive. They can lead to **overdose** and death.

A person experiencing paranoia has strong feelings of fear, anger, and mistrust. They are unable to relax and get in arguments easily.

Prescription pills might make a person feel calm and take away any pain. When people abuse prescription pills, they usually don't get the pills from a doctor. The pills are usually given to them by a friend or relative. Prescription drugs are powerful. They can be very addictive. People build up a tolerance quickly. Often, prescription pills stop having an effect. So people start trying other drugs, such as heroin.

The Social Impact

Drugs don't just harm a person's body. They can harm their social skills. Many people first try drugs with a group of friends. For many people, it's a one-time thing. But some people become addicted. Addicts stop hanging out with their friends. They spend more time alone or with other drug users. Drugs are expensive. It costs a lot of money to support a drug habit. An addiction to prescription pills can cost $75 a day. A cocaine addiction can cost six times that much. Users might lie or steal from those they love to pay for drugs. Even occasional drug use can change someone's thoughts, feelings, and abilities. The quality of their relationships can decrease quickly.

Cocaine, crack, and meth are stimulants. Stimulants make people feel more aware, energized, and excited. They can also make people feel paranoid and anxious. Sometimes stimulants lead to violent behavior. They can also lead to unhealthy weight loss, heart problems, strokes, and seizures. Club drugs such as ecstasy can also make people feel more energized and excited. Some club drugs make people feel drowsy and relaxed. All club drugs can lead to depression and addiction.

Drug overdose deaths in the United States over time

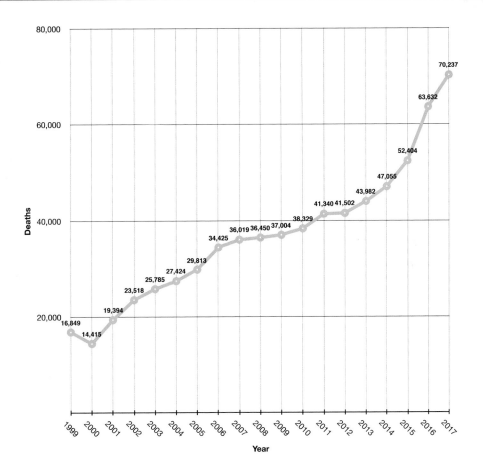

Dissociative drugs make people feel like they are separate from their body. These include ketamine, PCP, salvia, and certain cough and cold medicines. Dissociative drugs affect motor skills. They can also affect memory, coordination, and speech. LSD and mushrooms are examples of hallucinogens. Hallucinogens make people see things that aren't there, called hallucinations. Hallucinogens can affect people's emotions and make them feel nauseated. Most dissociative drugs and hallucinogens aren't as addictive as some other drugs.

The Culture of Drugs

*Modern **media** can make drug use seem normal or even glamorous. News of celebrities using drugs can be found online, on TV, and in magazines. Song lyrics and scenes in movies might make drug use seem cool. When coming across messages of drug use in the media, it is important to stop and think. You can ask yourself questions. How is this message trying to get my attention? How does it make me feel? How has it changed my thinking? What else do I know about this topic? Who created this message? What is the purpose of this message?*

Mild hallucinations include changes in light and sound. Intense hallucinations can include terrifying visions of beasts, melting walls, and cracks in people's faces.

CHAPTER 3

Teen Drug Use

Drugs are especially harmful to the teenage body. A teenager's body is growing. Their brain is still developing. When exposed to the chemicals in drugs, the brain does not develop properly. Brain damage can lead to problems with memory and problem-solving. The brain loses the ability to experience pleasure from normal life experiences.

A drug addiction is seriously disruptive to a teenager's life. Drug use can lead to poor performance at school. A teen drug user drops out of clubs and sports. They spend more and more time on the pursuit and usage of drugs. Relationships with friends and family go downhill. Teens have a higher risk of developing SUD than an adult. Teens that begin using

A 2018 study determined that the majority of eighth graders disapprove of both trying marijuana and smoking it occasionally.

drugs before age 15 are 6.5 times more likely to develop SUD than an adult.

There are many reasons why a teenager might decide to try drugs. Each person has their own thoughts, feelings, and experiences. There are some reasons teens have in common. Most often, teens try drugs for something to do. They are simply bored. Sometimes teens try drugs because they feel bad about themselves. They have low self-esteem or feel depressed. They think drugs will make them feel better. A teenager might try drugs because of curiosity. They want to feel something new.

Drug Use in Decline

Studies have shown that teen drug use has lessened in recent years. Marijuana is becoming more acceptable. But marijuana use by 8th and 10th graders is going down. Among high schoolers, cocaine, hallucinogens, and ecstasy use is going down too. Many experts think teens are replacing drugs with screens. Teens are spending more time on smartphones, computers, and video games. They are spending less time trying drugs. Apps, games, and the internet can make people feel good in the same way that many drugs do. A person can get addicted to screens just like they do drugs. Do you think there is a link between less drug use and more screen time?

There are also many social reasons why teens try drugs. A drug experience can be a way of bonding with friends.

Another reason behind teen drug use is peer pressure. Teens feel pressure differently than adults. Most adults don't care as much what others think about them. But many teenagers are very aware of their peers' opinions. When it comes to drugs, there are two types of pressure. Direct social pressure is when someone is offered drugs. Other people may be watching. Someone may be teased for saying no. Indirect pressure is when someone feels like they should try drugs just by being around them. No one is offering. No one is even paying attention. This type of pressure can be just as powerful. It is important for teenagers to think about the types of pressure they may be feeling.

Prescription Drug Use

Today, prescription drugs are very common. People get a prescription when they are sick, hurt, or have surgery. Prescription pills help people recover. But someone with a prescription might get addicted. A family member or friend might get unused pills and abuse them. Many people argue that prescription drugs are more dangerous than illicit drugs. Prescription pills are easier to get. They can be found in most homes. Other people think prescription pills can be safe. The pills just have to be used how a doctor says. Unused pills need to be disposed of properly. What do you think?

CHAPTER 4

Solving Drug Use

When struggling with drug problems, it can be hard for a person to get help. Many people with SUD are afraid of what other people will think. Or they don't know where to go or have a way to pay for **treatment**. Less than 20 percent of people with SUD seek treatment. It is possible to recover from SUD, but it is not easy. Many people with SUD fight it all their lives.

The first step to recovery is to get help. This starts with talking to someone. It can be a parent or other family member. Or it can be a guidance counselor or teacher. The conversation needs to feel safe and comfortable. Sometimes people do not feel comfortable talking to someone they know. They can find information in books or online first.

Millions of people seek recovery from drug addiction every year, and each person's recovery is different.

There are also hotlines that they can call for advice. The Substance Abuse and Mental Health Services Administration (SAMHSA) can be reached at 1-800-662-HELP (4357). This type of support is free and confidential.

People with SUD are usually helped at a treatment center. It may be a private business or a government program. While there, the person often stops using drugs for the first time. Their bodies are dependent on the drugs. They go through **withdrawal**. Withdrawal can be dangerous. Sometimes a patient is given prescription drugs to ease the transition.

The Warning Signs

There are many warning signs of substance use disorder. People at risk for SUD lose control of their drug use. They use more drugs than they planned, or for longer periods of time. They try to quit or use less, but cannot. Drug users' eyes might be bloodshot or glassy. They might have sudden weight change and problems sleeping. Their attitude and personality might change. They might be more angry and irritable. People at risk for SUD start to choose drugs over other things they like to do. They use drugs even if it causes problems with friends, family, work, school, or the law. It is important to be honest and aware of yourself and other people in your life. If you think you or a loved one might have a problem, reach out for help.

People going through the early days of recovery are very fragile. They need a lot of support. Professional counselors provide help and education. They share tools for leading a life without drugs.

There are about 70,000 Narcotics Anonymous
meetings held every week around the world.

Drug abuse counselors work in hospitals, mental health clinics, and private businesses. They receive special training and licenses to do their work.

After treatment, someone with SUD may still struggle. They might think about drugs and have urges to use them. Many people find being part of a support group helps. Cocaine Anonymous (CA) and Narcotics Anonymous (NA) hold meetings across the country. In these groups, people share their stories. They share ways to help maintain recovery. People often see a counselor for months or even years after SUD treatment ends.

Many people recover from SUD completely. The majority of people do not. Even with professional treatment and support groups, between 40 and 60 percent of people with SUD start using drugs again.

A Disease or a Choice?

Many people argue over what causes a person to become addicted to drugs. In the past, most people have thought it was a choice. A person chooses to try drugs. They then choose to keep using drugs, which can lead to addiction. Therefore, it is their fault if they get addicted. Today, many people think drug addiction is a disease. If a person has a brain disorder, even just trying a drug can cause addiction. This is not their fault. Addiction might run in their family too. Many people think a person with an addiction should not be blamed. People are not blamed for getting other diseases, such as cancer. What do you think are the strong and weak points behind each argument?

CHAPTER 5

Making Healthy Choices

Many people choose to do drugs at some point in their lives. Each time, they are taking a risk. Some people will be fine. Others will begin a lifelong battle with addiction. Only you can make choices for yourself. But you have to live with the results of those decisions. Choosing not to do drugs can be tough. You might lose friends if they choose to do drugs and you do not. You might have to work harder to find ways to stay busy.

Many teens try drugs because they are bored. Or they are looking for an exciting new experience. There are many ways to experience healthy risk-taking. Try rock climbing at a local gym or community center. Race go-karts with your friends. If you are not a physical person, risks can be taken creatively too. Learn a new art form or musical instrument. Read a scary

Healthy risk-taking releases adrenaline, a hormone that gives the body a boost of excitement and energy.

book. Join a club, take up a new hobby, or try out for a school play.

Teenagers may choose to try drugs because they are stressed or depressed. There are better ways to fix these problems. Healthy food choices and regular physical activity are essential. This doesn't have to mean hitting the gym three days a week. Activities such as dancing, hiking, and swimming for fun are options too. Creating a relaxing environment for yourself is important. This means turning off the TV and smartphone. Learn to be quiet and calm without distraction. Journaling can also be a helpful way to work through bad feelings.

Personal Goals

Drug use interrupts a person's life. Problems with drugs can interfere with someone's goals, leading to closed doors and missed opportunities. Write a list of your personal goals. The list should include short-term goals for the next few months. Your list should also have long-term goals for the next couple of years. Your long-term goals can also include your vision for adulthood. What do you want to do with your life? What do you want to accomplish? How could an addiction to drugs interfere with these goals?

When making decisions about drug use, it is important to think about the effects of drugs on the body and mind. It is important to know about the dangers and consequences of drug use. It is also important to think about your priorities. It is hard to find the **will** to stick to your priorities. But doing this over time builds inner strength.

Writing uses a different part of the brain than speaking. Many people communicate better through writing than talking.

Breaking the Habit

Breaking an addiction to drugs is very difficult. It takes courage, dedication, and hope. You can practice these skills by breaking a bad habit. First, find ways to decrease your stress. Stress can cause bad habits to form. What situations or feelings trigger your habit? Knowing your triggers can help you avoid them in the future. Replace your bad habit with a good habit that increases your health and happiness. Have a good reason for quitting. Reminding yourself of your reason can help you through difficult times. Envision your life without this bad habit and set goals. Visualization can lead to better outcomes. What other ideas do you have for ways to break a bad habit?

Science has shown that family support increases
the chance of recovery for people with SUD.

Think About It

Narcotics Anonymous was first started in 1953. It grew from Alcoholics Anonymous, which started in the 1940s. Today, NA includes people in 144 countries around the world. Millions of people with addictions have benefited from NA, AA, and similar groups.

While in NA or AA, members regularly attend meetings. They have a sponsor. A sponsor has been in recovery for a long time and acts as a mentor or guide. As part of their recovery, all members work through the 12 Steps. Use the internet or the library to research the 12 Steps. How do you think each step might help someone with their recovery? Why do you think NA and similar programs are successful?

Learn More

BOOKS

Abramovitz, Melissa. *Understanding Addiction.* Understanding Psychology. San Diego: ReferencePoint Press, Inc., 2018.

Baruch-Feldman, Caren. *The Grit Guide for Teens: A Workbook to Help You Build Perseverance, Self-Control, and a Growth Mindset.* Oakland: Instant Help Books, 2017.

Horning, Nicole. *Drug Abuse: Inside an American Epidemic.* New York: Lucent Press, 2018.

ON THE WEB

Above the Influence
https://abovetheinfluence.com

Kids' Health Goal Setting
http://www.cyh.com/HealthTopics/HealthTopicDetailsKids.aspx?p=335&id=2368

National Institute on Drug Abuse for Teens
https://teens.drugabuse.gov

Positive Choices
https://positivechoices.org.au/students

GLOSSARY

abuse (uh-BYOOSS) to misuse a substance in a way that harms the body

addiction (uh-DIK-shun) having no control over doing something, such as drugs or gambling, even though you know it is bad for your health and life

disorder (dis-OR-dur) a mental or physical illness

drug (DRUG) a substance that causes a chemical change in the body

euphoria (yew-FOR-ee-uh) an overwhelming feeling of happiness and contentment

high (HYE) the mental state caused by certain drugs, usually with feelings of calm and happiness

media (MEE-dee-uh) the ways that messages are made available to large groups of people, including newspapers, TV shows, movies, and music

overdose (OH-vur-dohss) taking enough drugs to become ill or die

tolerance (TALL-ehr-entz) the ability to put up with something that is harmful or difficult

treatment (TREET-muhnt) a plan to help someone heal from a sickness or addiction, usually including medication or therapy

will (WIL) the power of the mind to decide a course of action and follow through with it

withdrawal (with-DRAW-ul) the painful and unpleasant physical reaction experienced when quitting drugs

INDEX